Katie Ledecky
Swimming's Golden Girl

Katie Ledecky
Swimming's Golden Girl

By Mario Petrrino

Creative Media Publishing

CREATIVE MEDIA, INC.
PO Box 6270
Whittier, California 90609-6270
United States of America

www.creativemedia.net

Book & cover design by Joseph Dzidrums

First Edition: May 2016

Library of Congress Control Number
On File

Print ISBN	eBook ISBN
978-1-938438-54-7	978-1-938438-55-4

To SB Sonia

Table of Contents

"I've just always felt comfortable in the water from day one."

On March 17, 1997, in Washington, D.C., David and Mary Gen Ledecky welcomed their daughter into the world. The thankful parents named their bundle of joy Kathleen Genevieve Ledecky. The happy father and mother were already raising a three-year-old son named Michael and felt thrilled to add a little girl to their growing family. The parents began calling their daughter "Katie" and the nickname stuck.

Swimming ran in Katie's family. Her mother was a competitive swimmer for the University of New Mexico. She still loved her former sport dearly.

Right before Katie's sixth birthday, USA Swimming held a national event in Maryland. The Ledeckys were thrilled to watch a high-level competition in their home state. Katie felt exhilarated by the sights and sounds of competitive swimming.

After the competition ended, Katie approached several swimmers hoping to speak with her heroes. Michael Phelps, Team USA's top athlete, thrilled her by giving her his autograph. In fact, the young swimmer met many of her idols that day.

Naturally, Katie's brother began swimming at a young age. At age six, Katie followed him into the pool. Not surprisingly, the Ledecky children were outstanding swimmers with natural talent. Water felt like a second home to the active siblings.

The Ledeckys lived in Bethesda, Maryland, an affluent area in Montgomery County. *Forbes Magazine* once dubbed their hometown: America's "most educated" small town. With its picturesque setting and low crime rate, parents regarded Bethesda as a desirable community to raise children.

Katie joined Nation's Capital Swim Club, an association that boasted a top coaching staff. Yuri Suguiyama, a former competitive swimmer, trained the young girl. The accomplished athlete acclimated quickly to the water sport, rapidly advancing past students who were much older than her.

By the time Katie reached her teen years, she swam competitively for Team USA and competed on Stone Ridge School of the Sacred Heart's swim team. Competing on two levels while going to school full time proved challenging, but the youngster wouldn't have it any other way.

Katie felt determined to remain in a traditional school environment. She wanted the complete high school experience. By the end of her high school career, Katie had set records in every event except the 100-yard breaststroke.

To most people, Katie seemed like an ordinary teenager who balanced swimming with a traditional school experience. However, she kept improving every day. The world would soon discover that the athlete was anything but common.

"My faith has always been important to me. It defines who I am."

The 2012 United States Olympic Trials marked Katie's first senior national competition. The eager participant landed in Omaha, Nebraska, with little fanfare. After all, only junior competitions filled her short resume.

Each event's top finishers would advance to the London Olympics. Every athlete dreamed of competing on the biggest sports stage in the world. Katie was no exception.

Sunday, July 1, 2012. That's the day when Katie Ledecky's life changed forever. In the 800-meter freestyle, the trials' youngest swimmer completed the race with a scorching time of 8 minutes 19.78 seconds.

When her hand touched the wall, Katie threw off her goggles and scanned the scoreboard to find her final placement.

First! Katie had won the event. In fact, the talented teenager had finished an entire two seconds over second-place swimmer Kate Ziegler, a former world champion in the grueling event. The fifteen-year-old grinned broadly and pumped her fist triumphantly at her unbelievable achievement.

Thanks to her first-place finish, Katie made the 2012 Olympic team! The unassuming teenager felt elated. Four years earlier, she hadn't even known how the Olympic qualifying process worked. Now she would represent Team USA in London.

"I never told myself I had (first place)," she told *The Washington Post.* "I just kept trying to hold the same pace."

Katie's friends and family were equally thrilled with her accomplishment. Her parents and brother cheered heartily upon the realization that the youngest Ledecky was Olympic bound. They were thrilled that the teenager would get the rare opportunity to compete on sport's most prestigious stage. The close-knit family knew how hard the swimmer had worked over the years to juggle a burgeoning athletic career with a difficult academic schedule.

Longtime coach Yuri Suguiyama became quite emotional when reflecting on his student's victory. He found it heartwarming to watch a kind, hard worker excel in the sport. Her placement was a nice reminder that nice girls could finish first.

"(Katie's) a 15-year-old lady who comes to the pool every day with a smile on her face and an unbelievable work ethic," Yuri told *The Washington Post*. "I was just really proud, really happy for her. She earned it."

Meanwhile, silver medalist Kate Ziegler studied the youthful champion thoughtfully. The former world champion liked the talented girl.

Katie clearly had a sensible head on her shoulders, and she did not present a diva attitude. At that moment, the veteran Olympian decided to mentor Katie. Her Olympic experience could prove to be valuable to the rookie swimmer.

After her unexpected victory, an avalanche of media exposure descended upon Katie. Reporters raced to interview the surprise winner. Everyone wanted to become acquainted with the new Olympian. They fired questions at her.

When did you begin swimming?

Did you expect to make the team?

Can you win a medal in London?

Will you go sightseeing in the U.K.?

Every day for weeks, members of the press requested interviews with Katie. Family and friends called the Ledecky child to extend their congratulations. Even complete strangers approached Katie to praise her for making the Olympic team. Sometimes, they also offered words of encouragement.

"Go for the gold," people often told the teeenager.

Mostly, though, whether people were family, media, or strangers, they asked Katie the same question over and over.

How does it feel to qualify for the Olympic Games?

The teen often exclaimed, "It's unreal; It's unbelievable."

*"I set goals from
a very early age,
and that's what's led
to my success."*

2012 Olympic prognosticators predicted that Michael Phelps, Missy Franklin, and Ryan Lochte would capture gold medals for USA Swimming. Indeed, the three athletes performed exceedingly well amassing 16 medals between them. The biggest surprise? A relative unknown girl from Maryland joined the American celebration.

Before the Olympics, the United States swim team gathered to film a music video set to the smash single "Call Me Maybe." Katie and her American teammates bonded while lipsynching to Carly Rae Jepson's catchy pop tune. When USA Swimming uploaded the video to their official *YouTube* channel, it swiftly went viral. By the time the London Games began, most people had seen the recording or heard about it. Not surprisingly, the video received over 14 million views!

When Katie arrived in London, England, people recognized her for two reasons. One, the newcomer was the surprise winner of the 800-meter at trials. Two, at 15 years, 4 months, and 10 days, she was Team USA's youngest member.

The 2012 Summer Olympics swimming competitions began on July 28. The sport featured 34 events with an even split of male and female events. The Aquatics Centre hosted 32 meets; Hyde Park hosted two 10 kilometer open-water competitions.

The Olympic 800-meter event marked Katie's first senior international competition. That knowledge would be stressful for any athlete to handle. Yet, the teenager was mature behind her years. Instead of wilting from stress, she embraced the intense pressure like a confident, seasoned professional.

Superstar Rebecca Adlington was the overwhelming favorite to win the gold medal in the 800-meter competition. After all, the home country favorite was the event's reigning world and Olympic champion. For several months, the legendary swimmer had dominated newspaper headlines all over England. Most fans of the sport expected that the popular athlete would cruise to victory, especially with the encouragement and goodwill of the London crowd behind her.

Moments before the 800-meter, the competitors marched onto the pool deck to warm up. In a few minutes, one swimmer would land in the history books by capturing Olympic gold. The British crowd roared for Rebecca.

"Becky, Becky, Becky," they chanted.

Meanwhile, Katie's cheering section wasn't too shabby either. Her backers included Michael Phelps, the most decorated Olympian ever. The superstar had stopped the teen backstage to offer encouragement and a high five.

Some competitors listened to inspirational music before a big race. Not Katie, though. Sure, the fifteen-year-old loved rock music, especially Bruce Springsteen, but she liked preparing for a competition in silence. The peaceful environment and lack of distractions kept her calm while she visualized what she wanted to accomplish in the pool.

Finally, an official summoned the competitors to the pool. It was finally race time!

The toned athletes stood in front of their respective lanes. They struck their start position and waited for the signal to start the race.

Bang!

Katie began her Olympic dream by jumping into lane three and immediately secured first place. She kept the lead for 750 meters.

With 50 meters remaining, the Ledeckys realized Katie could win the gold medal. They shouted encouraging words to the youngest family member. Even the pro-Rebecca crowd cheered for Katie. They were impressed that she hadn't once acquiesced the lead.

When the American finally touched the wall, she surveyed her surroundings. Katie won the gold medal by more than four seconds over Spain's Mireia Belmonte Garcia. Rebecca rounded out the podium in third place.

Katie grinned while her family celebrated in the stands. Several competitors congratulated the teenager, including Rebecca, who admired the amazing feat.

"Unbelievable," she gushed about Katie. "Fantastic. Absolutely amazing."

"It's one of the biggest shocks I've ever seen in the Olympics," USA Swimming National Team Director Frank Busch remarked. "Stuff like this just doesn't happen."

After an exhilarating medal ceremony, Katie faced a bevy of impressed reporters. She wore a shiny new souvenir and an even bigger smile.

Although Katie's Olympic gold medal was the first international senior medal she had won, Katie was not shocked by her historic victory. She had always believed in herself,

"I knew if I put my mind to it, I could do it," Katie remarked honestly to *The Washington Post*. "I wasn't intimidated at all."

Katie had shown confidence in the biggest competition of her life! She had a stunning new gold medal to prove it.

"I continue to train like I didn't go to the Olympics and win gold, that I still have a lot to accomplish and that keeps memotivated and excited."

Following the Olympics, wellwishers welcomed Katie home at Dulles International Airport. Television cameras captured the celebration and broadcast it on the evening news. Some fans waved homemade signs while others presented thoughtful gifts to the Olympic champion.

The grateful swimmer seemed surprised by the large turnout. Touched to see so many supporters, she smiled brightly and thanked her fans for their encouragement. Despite being exhausted by a thrilling Olympic experience and long plane ride home, the champion signed autographs and posed for photos for a long time.

For the next several weeks, Katie reminisced about her London experience on radio and television shows. She also granted interviews to several magazines and newspapers. The thoughtful fifteen-year-old even delighted children by visiting local schools; Students lined up just to touch her gold medal.

Katie's remarkable Olympic accomplishment earned her many new fans and countless accolades. The teenager's fan mail skyrocketed, and her social media prescence received a healthy boost of followers. Later that year, she won two Golden Goggle Awards.

In November of 2012, Katie resumed training full time. Yet, she now had someone different guiding her. After Yuri Suguiyama accepted California State University's offer to join their coaching staff, the Olympic champion turned to former competitive swimmer Bruce Gemmell for guidance. New coach and student instantly clicked.

"She and her family were so welcoming to me, and although she was initially apprehensive about changing up her training, she quickly realized the changes I proposed would make her a faster distance swimmer," Gemmell explained to *USA Swimming*.

Following the 2012 Olympics, Katie emerged as swimming's newest star. The teenager handled her newfound celebrity effortlessly. Yet, people wondered how she would handle the pressure of being the overwhelming favorite to win competitions.

Lucky for Katie, she possessed an optimistic attitude combined with sturdy determination. The teenager dismissed any speculation that she might wilt under scrutiny or weighty expectations. Sure, she may have already won Olympic gold, but it felt like her career was just getting started!

"It's a great feeling to know that I can do something great that can impact others."

In July, Katie traveled to Barcelona, Spain, for the 2013 World Aquatic Championships. The scenic city that rests on the Mediterranean coast had experience holding major sporting events. Over twenty years earlier, the tourist destination had hosted the 1992 Barcelona Olympics.

Katie competed in three individual events at worlds: the 1,500, 800, and 400-meter freestyle. She also participated in the 4x200 freestyle relay. The teen won all four events. In the 1,500 meter, she crushed the world record by six seconds.

So, what did Katie do for an encore at the next world championships? She nabbed five gold medals setting three new world records in the process. The plucky teenager won the 200, 400, 800 and 1500, and the 4×200-meter freestyle.

Two years after the London Olympics, Katie had undergone an amazing transformation. The once promising upstart had become the world's most dominant female swimmer.

"Every race is a sprint. Some races are just longer sprints than others."

College Dreams

Like most high school juniors, Katie thought about college a lot. Unlike most teenagers, though, the now seventeen-year-old had full-scholarship offers from several esteemed universities. Numerous colleges offered the swimming sensation a free education if she competed for their swim team. The collegiate swimming world followed Katie's impending college announcement intently. Sports fans clamored to learn where she intended to study.

On May 15, 2014, Katie declared her college decision via a widely-circulated press release. In the end, there was much celebration in Mountain View, California.

"I am thrilled to announce that upon completion of my high school education, I am committed to pursuing my education at Stanford and very much look forward to the opportunity to swim for the Stanford Cardinal women's team in NCAA competition.

"I am very excited about the educational opportunities that will be available to me at Stanford and to swim for its great NCAA program under the leadership of Coach Greg Meehan and Assistant Coach Tracy Duchac.

"I always knew I wanted to swim collegiately and have that experience," Katie later told *NPR*. "I've heard so many great things about competing in the NCAA. I think it's the best decision for myself. I think that way I will continue to improve."

A high school honors student, Katie felt confident about balancing swimming with college studies. Meanwhile, Stanford welcomed the Olympic champion with open arms.

Katie had entered the 2012 London Olympics as a relative unknown. Team USA's rookie shocked sports fans with her Olympic victory. Yet, much can change in four years.

A different Katie will compete at the 2016 Games, though. She will seek a second consecutive title in the 1500 meter but plans to pursue gold in numerous other events, too.

Expectations are high for the world's best swimmer in 2016. However, whatever happens in Rio, Katie has already established herself as one of America's all-time greatest swimmers. Anything else she achieves will merely strengthen her already magnificent legacy.

"I want to embrace the Olympic theme of inspiring a generation," Katie once told *USA Swimming*.

She has already accomplished that goal.

Essential Katie Links

Official Facebook Page
www.facebook.com/KatieLedecky

Official Twitter Page
www.Twitter.com/katieledecky

Official Instagram Account
www.instagram.com/kledecky

USA Swimming
www.usaswimming.org

Team USA
www.teamusa.org

Rio 2016
www.rio2016.com

Competitive Record

Women's 800 Meter Freestyle Olympic Champions

2016 Rio de Janeiro		
2012 London	Katie Ledecky	USA
2008 Beijing	Rebecca Adlington	GBR
2004 Athens	Ai Shibata	JPN
2000 Sydney	Brooke Bennett	USA
1996 Atlanta	Brooke Bennett	USA
1992 Barcelona	Janet Evans	USA
1988 Seoul	Janet Evans	USA
1984 Los Angeles	Tiffany Cohen	USA
1980 Moscow	Michelle Ford	AUS
1976 Montreal	Petra Thümer	GDR
1972 Innsbruck	Kenna Rothhamme	USA
1968 Mexico City	Debbie Meye	USA

2012 Olympics

London, England — July 28 - August 10, 2012 — 800-Mᴇᴛᴇʀ Fʀᴇᴇsᴛʏʟᴇ

Gold	Katie Ledecky	United States	8:14.63
Silver	Mireia Belmonte García	Spain	8:18.76
Bronze	Rebecca Adlington	Great Britain	8:20.32
4	Lauren Boyle	New Zealand	8:22.72
5	Lotte Friis	Denmark	8:23.86
6	Boglárka Kapás	Hungary	8:23.89
7	Coralie Balmy	France	8:29.26
8	Andreina Pinto	Venezuela	8:29.28

Competitive Record

2015 World Aquatic Championships
KAZAN, RUSSIA — JULY 24 - AUGUST 9, 2015

Women's 1500-Meter Freestyle

1	Katie Ledecky	United States	15:25.48
2	Lauren Boyle	New Zealand	15:40.14
3	Boglárka Kapás	Hungary	15:47.09
4	Lotte Friis	Denmark	15:49.00
5	Jessica Ashwood	Australia	15:52.17
6	Sharon van Rouwendaal	Netherlands	16:03.74
7	Kristel Köbrich	Chile	16:06.55
8	Aurora Ponsele	Italy	16:09.57

Women's 800-Meter Freestyle

1	Katie Ledecky	United States	8:07.39
2	Lauren Boyle	New Zealand	8:17.65
3	Jazmin Carlin	Great Britain	8:18.15
4	Jessica Ashwood	Australia	8:18.41
5	Lotte Friis	Denmark	8:21.36
6	Boglárka Kapás	Hungary	8:22.93
7	Sarah Köhler	Germany	8:23.67
8	Sharon van Rouwendaal	Netherlands	8:24.12

Women's 400-Meter Freestyle

1	Katie Ledecky	United States	3:59.13
2	Sharon van Rouwendaal	Netherlands	4:03.02
3	Jessica Ashwood	Australia	4:03.34
4	Jazmin Carlin	Great Britain	4:03.74
5	Lauren Boyle	New Zealand	4:04.38
6	Melania Costa	Spain	4:06.50
7	Diletta Carli	Italy	4:07.30
8	Boglárka Kapás	Hungary	4:08.22

Women's 200-Meter Freestyle

1	Katie Ledecky	United States	1:55.16
2	Federica Pellegrini	Italy	1:55.32
3	Missy Franklin	United States	1:55.49
4	Veronika Popova	Russia	1:56.16
5	Katinka Hosszú	Hungary	1:56.19
6	Shen Duo	China	1:56.27
7	Emma McKeon	Australia	1:56.41
8	Femke Heemskerk	Netherlands	1:56.79

About the Publisher

Creative Media Publishing has produced biographies on several inspiring personalities: *Simone Biles, Nadia Comaneci, Clayton Kershaw, Mike Trout, Yuna Kim, Shawn Johnson, Nastia Liukin, The Fierce Five, Gabby Douglas, Sutton Foster, Kelly Clarkson, Idina Menzel, Missy Franklin* and more. They've published two award-winning Young Adult novels, *Cutters Don't Cry* (Moonbeam Children's Book Award) and *Kaylee: The "What If?" Game* (Children's Literary Classic Awards). They have also produced a line of popular children's book series, including *The Creeper and the Cat*, *Future Presidents Club*, *Princess Dessabelle* and *Quinn: The Balleria*.

www.CreativeMedia.net
@CMIPublishing

Now sports fans can learn about gymnastics' greatest stars! Americans **Shawn Johnson** and **Nastia Liukin** became the darlings of the 2008 Beijing Olympics when the fearless gymnasts collected 9 medals between them. Four years later at the 2012 London Olympics, America's **Fab Five** claimed gold in the team competition. A few days later, **Gabby Douglas** added another gold medal to her collection when she became the fourth American woman in history to win the Olympic all-around title. The *GymnStars* series reveals these gymnasts' long, arduous path to Olympic glory. *Gabby Douglas: Golden Smile, Golden Triumph* received a **2012 Moonbeam Children's Book Award**.

At the 2010 Vancouver Olympics, tragic circumstances thrust **Joannie Rochette** into the spotlight when her mother died two days before the ladies short program. Joannie then captured hearts everywhere by courageously skating two moving programs to win the Olympic bronze medal. *Joannie Rochette: Canadian Ice Princess* profiles the popular figure skater's moving journey.

Meet figure skating's biggest star: **Yuna Kim**. The Korean trailblazer produced two legendary performances at the 2010 Vancouver Olympic Games to win the gold medal. *Yuna Kim: Ice Queen* uncovers the compelling story of how the beloved figure skater overcame poor training conditions, various injuries and numerous other obstacles to become world and Olympic champion.

Our *YNot Girl* series chronicles the lives and careers of the world's most famous role models. *Jennie Finch: Softball Superstar* details the California native's journey from a shy youngster to softball's most famous face. In *Kelly Clarkson: Behind Her Hazel Eyes*, young readers will find inspiration reading about the superstar's rise from a broke waitress with big dreams to becoming one of the recording industry's top musical acts. *Missy Franklin: Swimming Sensation* narrates the Colorado native's transformation from a talented swimming toddler to queen of the pool.

Theater fans first fell for **Sutton Foster** in her triumphant turn as *Thoroughly Modern Millie*. Since then the triple threat has charmed Broadway audiences by playing a writer, a princess, a movie star, a nightclub singer, and a Transylvania farm girl. Now the two-time Tony winner is conquering television in the acclaimed series *Bunheads*. A children's biography, *Sutton Foster: Broadway Sweetheart, TV Bunhead* details the role model's rise from a tiny ballerina to the toast of Broadway and Hollywood.

Idina Menzel's career has been "Defying Gravity" for years! With starring roles in *Wicked* and *Rent*, the Tony-winner is one of theater's most beloved performers. The powerful vocalist has also branched out in other mediums. She has filmed a recurring role on television's smash hit *Glee* and lent her talents to the Disney films, *Enchanted* and *Frozen*. A children's biography, *Idina Menzel: Broadway Superstar* narrates the actress' rise to fame from a Long Island wedding singer to overnight success!

Fair Youth
Emylee of Forest Springs

Twelve-year-old Emylee Markette has felt invisible her entire life. Then one fateful afternoon, three beautiful sisters arrive in her sleepy New England town and instantly become the most popular girls at Forest Springs Middle School. To everyone's surprise, the Fay sisters befriend Emylee and welcome her into their close-knit circle. Before long, the shy loner finds herself running with the cool crowd, joining the track team and even becoming friends with her lifelong crush.

Through it all, though, Emylee's weighed down by nagging suspicions. Why were the Fay sisters so anxious to befriend her? How do they know some of her inner thoughts? What do they truly want from her?

When Emylee eventually discovers that her new friends are secretly fairies, she finds her life turned upside down yet again and must make some life-changing decisions.

Fair Youth: Emylee of Forest Springs marks the first volume in an exciting new book series.

Ashley Moore wants to know why there's never been a girl president. Before long the inspired six-year-old creates a special, girls-only club - the **Future Presidents Club**. Meet five enthusiastic young girls who are ready to change the world. *Future Presidents Club: Girls Rule* is the first book in a series about girls making a difference!

Meet **Princess Dessabelle**, a spoiled, lonely princess with a quick temper.

In *Princess Dessabelle Makes a Friend,* the lonely youngster discovers the meaning of true friendship. *Princess Dessabelle: Tennis Star* finds the pampered girl learning the importance of good sportsmanship.

Quinn the Ballerina can hardly believe it's finally performance day. She's playing her first principal role in a production of *The Sleeping Beauty*.

Yet, Quinn is also nervous. Can she really dance the challenging steps? Will people believe her as a cursed princess caught in a 100-year spell?

Join Quinn as she transforms into Princess Aurora in an exciting retelling of Tchaikovsky's *The Sleeping Beauty*. Now you can relive, or experience for the first time, one of ballet's most acclaimed works as interpreted by a 9 year old.

2010 Moonbeam Children's Book Award Winner! In a series of raw journal entries written to her absentee father, a teenager chronicles her penchant for self-harm, a serious struggle with depression and an inability to vocally express her feelings.

"I play the 'What If?'" game all the time. It's a cruel, wicked game."

When free spirit Kaylee suffers a devastating loss, her personality turns dark as she struggles with depression and un-resolved anger. Can Kaylee repair her broken spirit, or will she remain a changed person?

Winning Silver

What happens when Elise delivers perfect routines but doesn't win? Can the disappointed gymnast accept the silver medal when she dreamed only of gold?

Filled with adorable illustrations and armed with straightforward storytelling, **Winning Silver** stresses the importance of good sportsmanship. Anyone who has ever felt gutted by a competitive result will relate to Elise's initial disappointment over not getting the result she expected.

From the popular new series, *Classical Reboots,* ***Rapunzel*** updates the **Brothers Grimm** fairy tale with hilarious and heartbreaking results.

Rapunzel has been locked in her adoptive mother's attic for years. Just as the despondent teenager abandons hope of escaping her private prison, a mysterious tablet computer appears. Before long, Rapunzel's quirky fairy godmother, Aiko, has the conflicted young girl questioning her place in the world.

Made in the USA
Lexington, KY
22 September 2016